Blessing Your Enemies, Forgiving Your Friends

A Scriptural Journey Into Personal Peace

Kristen Johnson Ingram

LIGUORI
PUBLICATIONS

One Liguori Drive
Liguori, MO 63057-9999
(314) 464-2500

ISBN 0-89243-523-2
Library of Congress Catalog Card Number: 93-77038

Copyright © 1993, Kristen Johnson Ingram
Printed in the United States of America

Scripture quotations are taken from THE NEW AMERICAN BIBLE WITH REVISED NEW TESTAMENT, copyright © 1986, AND THE REVISED PSALMS, copyright © 1991, by the Confraternity of Christian Doctrine, Washington, D.C., and are used with permission. All rights reserved.

The Bible quotations on pages 20 and 69 are taken from THE NEW REVISED STANDARD VERSION (NRSV), copyright © 1989, Division of Christian Education of the National Council of the Churches of Christ in the United States of America. Used with permission. All rights reserved.

Cover design by Chris Sharp

Contents

Introduction

I had been praying for my enemies all my life—praying for them to change, that is. One day God focused my attention on Jesus' words that admonish me to *bless* my enemies instead of trying to get God to make them behave.

I began stammering a prayer for someone I disliked very much, praying that the person would be blessed that day with special success in business and personal happiness.

Does that sound radical? It is. Christianity is a radical lifestyle. Jesus wasn't crucified because he pandered to the temple hierarchy. He wasn't put to death because he counseled me to do what is natural: to get even, to punish offenders, to hate people that hate me and love those that love and admire me. Jesus asked me to do just the opposite of what is natural: to pray for my enemies' happiness and success. As a conscientious Christian, I have no choice but to obey.

After that first faltering prayer, I began to search my heart for old enmities, old resentments, and unforgiven offenses. I've always thought of myself as a pretty forgiving person—not one who holds grudges or nurses emotional wounds. But when I began to reach deep into my psyche, I discovered a wastebasket of unforgiveness. In fact, the exercise became a game for me, to see what old annoyance I could dredge up and what old enemy I could bless and forgive.

Sometimes I discovered that the hurt didn't disappear just because I forgave the person. I had to bless those enemies as well.

Gradually, my life changed. I don't mean that everyone I prayed for expressed remorse for their wrongdoing; I don't mean that it was easy to forgive certain persons, like child molesters, crooked politicians, and people who continued to hurt or anger me. I did witness a few small miracles, however. Primarily, my spiritual journey into peace changed. I became more willing to recognize my own sins and my need for forgiveness. I realized that Jesus' words about blessing your enemies were ultimately meant to benefit me—as are all God's commandments.

The prayer of blessing affects the pray-er and the person prayed for as well. I was upset at some family members who had been unreasonable and spiteful; they spurned our every attempt to talk with them. Eventually, they withdrew altogether and didn't speak to us at all. They scorned our company, ignored our birthdays, and dismissed the gifts we sent them and their son.

For two years, I asked God to intervene, to change the situation, to soften the harshness at the center of this young family. Nothing changed.

One day soon after God called my attention to the prayer of blessing, I was impelled to try a different kind of prayer. "God, please bless John and Frances today. Give them a feast of a day. Let the sun shine on them. Let them go out to dinner or a movie and have a wonderful time."

About nine o'clock that evening, we received a long-distance call. It was John and Frances. "Life is too short for this. We're flying in tomorrow to see you, if that's okay."

A miracle, yes, but a small one. The big miracle had occurred within me. Long before we got that phone call, I had been blessed. As I prayed for that family's peace and prosperity, I changed; I became a stronger, better person. God's blessings encircled me; the miracle of the phone call was secondary.

Blessing Your Enemies, Forgiving Your Friends is an adventure in scriptural living, a mile-by-mile discovery of what prayer and reconciliation really are.

How to Use this Book

As you work through this book, you will mark many milestones in your spiritual journey. Each chapter opens with a Scripture reference that lays the wisdom of God before your heart. I suggest you check the Scripture reference in your own Bible, write it on a small piece of paper, and post it where you'll see it frequently as you work on that particular chapter. Because the material in this book is Scripture-based, you will want to keep your Bible nearby at all times.

"Prayer" follows the Scripture reference. This brief invocation helps you embrace your own neediness and hold it before God's loving gaze.

The theme of each chapter is then capsulized in "The Teaching." This brief summary pinpoints the focus of that chapter and gives you a sense of direction as you follow the material.

Each chapter contains workbook material, stories, self-examination questions, and spiritual exercises that will help you on your journey of blessing and forgiving.

Each chapter ends with two blank pages. You can comment on your prayer life, insights, or form your own blessings and prayers. Although you may hesitate with this journaling exercise, trust yourself. Make this book your personal friend, and share yourself with its pages. Two pages is not an overwhelming space. If it isn't enough space, use a notebook. Expression is the purpose. Journaling is psychologically supportive and spiritually beneficial. It often exposes the heart's deepest shadows.

1.

"Lord, Who Is My Enemy?"

> LORD, you have probed me, you know me:
> you know when I sit and stand,
> you understand my thoughts from afar.
> Psalm 139:1

Prayer

O God, you have not asked me to deny having enemies but
have directed me to acknowledge, bless, and forgive them.
Grant me the strength and courage to look inside myself.

Amen

The Teaching

Before we can begin to bless and forgive our enemies, we
have to recognize the hatreds and resentments we have
hidden from ourselves. With frequent use of the above
prayer, you can explore your heart for those quiet pockets
of anger and unforgiveness that may be doing you harm.

The following Examination of Heart will help you assess your
starting point. Several times throughout the book, you will work
through an exercise like this. For privacy and convenience, you may
want to record your responses in a separate notebook. Save your
responses, however, to help you chart your spiritual progress.

Examination of Heart

Some of the following statements may seem irrelevant to forgiveness. Nonetheless, honestly respond with "true" (T) or "false" (F) to each statement. You will eventually see how all statements connect to your personal situation.

1. T F I have absolutely no resentment, anger, bitterness or hatred toward people in my past or present life.

2. T F There is someone I have tried unsuccessfully to forgive.

3. T F There is someone I think I have forgiven—but I still feel hurt, anger, and bitterness toward that person.

4. T F I find myself easily irritated at inefficient, "stupid" clerks, salespeople, waitresses, gas station attendants, and so forth.

5. T F I think I feel resentment toward one or both of my parents for things that happened in my childhood.

6. T F Some of my teachers in school were unfair, even cruel to me.

7. T F When I was a child, I was "good-tempered"; I didn't argue with my parents, teachers, or friends. Although I always went along with things, I was sometimes mad inside.

8. T F Someone in my past or recent life cheated me out of money, recognition, a job, or a relationship.

9. T F I can't stand to have people angry at me.

10. T F Sometimes I daydream about showing people that I'm smarter than they thought, or about getting even with someone for past hurts.

Being Honest With God

Timmy Carville, his jeans torn and caked with mud, hurls himself through the living-room door. A trickle of blood has dried under his nose and the hole in his pants reveals a skinned knee.

"I hate Jason!" the nine-year-old rages as his mother helps him clean up. "I wish he would move away—far away."

Connie Carville sighs. Jason is, indeed, a cruel bully. But Connie is a devout Christian, and she hopes to teach her son that love is better than hate.

"Oh, Tim, you don't really hate Jason; you don't hate anyone," Connie says, dabbing a washcloth at Tim's upper lip. "You don't like what Jason does, but you love him. Let's pray for Jason."

"Okay," Tim agrees. "God, I hate Jason. Please make him move far away from here. Amen."

"Now, Tim, you do not hate Jason," his mother insists. "God wants you to love everyone."

Little does Connie realize that she is teaching her young son to deny and bury his anger. Fortunately, Tim's prayer is honest. He confesses hatred and anger and petitions God for help—something the rest of us have a hard time doing. Perhaps we can't approve of Tim's words, but we can admire his forthrightness and his ability to state his needs.

When Connie tells her young son that God wants us to love everyone, she is right, of course; God calls us to love. But God doesn't want us to pretend to love or to hide our emotions—even from ourselves.

"Lord, who is my neighbor?" the lawyer asks. In response, Jesus tells the parable of the Good Samaritan. What if the lawyer had asked, "Lord, who is my enemy?" Is my enemy the person I can vividly recall hurting me? my parent? pastor? sibling? spouse? child? coworker? Yes.

The Wedges of Memory

It is possible, however, that you've buried some enemies over the years. The pie graph below shows how much recall ability the mind has. Only about ten percent of human memory is conscious, waiting to be picked up. That mere ten percent helps you remember your dog's name and your spouse's face.

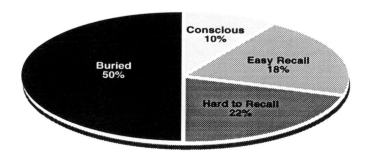

Approximately eighteen percent of human memory requires a nudge: "Remember when we went to the shore? Well, remember that bird we saw? Remember, a *red* bird?" With this kind of specific mental jogging, you can usually recall incidents or people. Prayer helps you recall things from this portion of your memory; so do the stimuli of names, places, smells, and so forth.

It may surprise you to discover that the biggest chunk of memory is deeply buried. Some of that is God's wisdom; we wouldn't be able to think at all if our conscious mind were cluttered with memory. But some of it is buried because we want it that way. Some persons and places in our past are so painful to remember that God provides a way for us to hide them.

Most of us don't need to probe deeply into these hidden recesses of the mind—unless it's obvious that we're angry at someone we can't quite remember.

Ask God to reveal to you the person or persons you resent or hate or feel wounded by. After meditation and searching, write the name or names that come to mind.

_____ _____

_____ _____

_____ _____

_____ _____

If you need more room, continue in your journal or in your notebook.

Do you know why you are so angry? List three incidents or factors that have left you hurt and resentful.

1. _____

_____

2. _____

_____

3. _____

_____

Where do you feel your anger? Is it in your stomach or behind your breastbone? Do you grind your teeth? Do you get a headache when you're with or think about certain people? What spot on your body signals rage or resentment?

_____

_____

_____

How long have you held this anger, knowingly or unknowingly?

Record a date or a period when you probably began to be resentful.

Date _____

Record anything else about the person or persons who generate anger in you: the unfairness with which he/she/they treated you, the way he/she/they rejected your affections, the times he/she/they embarrassed you. This list can be as long as you like. Don't excuse the person or yourself, or mince any words about your feelings.

_____

_____

_____

_____

_____

_____

"Lord, Is It I?"

Sometimes we meet the enemy and see ourselves. Are you familiar with that sudden, prickly irritation that can sweep over you in the presence of another person, a person you don't have any reason to dislike?

In the fourteenth century, Thomas à Kempis (*The Imitation of Christ*) pointed out what modern psychologists know today: the flaw in another person that causes us irritation or annoyance is usually something unacceptable in ourselves. Psychologists call this "projection"; Thomas à Kempis called it "sin." Whatever it is called, it can seriously impede Christian life. This kind of hidden self-hatred is often connected to spouse abuse: some persons hate themselves so much that they despise anyone who would stoop to loving and marrying them.

If you have been abused verbally, emotionally, physically, or sexually, you may need to get professional help to recognize and deal with the enemy within yourself. The irritation or annoyance that we associate with another, however, may simply indicate that we need to work on our own sins.

Recognition—But Not Action

The basic key to loving and praying for the people you can't stand is *recognition.* This is the first step in healing hatred, resentment, or simple irritation—recent or from the past.

The second great principle of relieving inner hatred is the realization that *you don't have to act out your anger.* Get in touch with it; peek under your own helmet to see just how mad you are. It's even okay to consider all the things you'd like to tell that person. But it's not okay to act on your anger—at least not until you finish this book. Give confession and prayer a chance.

As you recognize your anger, do so within the context of genuine love. In dealing with her son, for example, Connie's best course might be to let Tim express his feelings and then affirm his feelings with comments like "I can see that you're really mad at Jason" and "You think it's unfair that he gets away with beating you up."

Once Tim exhausts his anger and lets his emotional battery run down, Connie can help him understand why Jason behaves the way he does. Connie can help her young son find ways to turn his anger into constructive resolutions. Paul reminds us to "be angry, and sin not." Anger isn't the sin; the sin is what you do about it.

Confession

The step after recognition is to *confess your hatred as sin*. In the following space, acknowledge your stored-up hatred as sin.

_____

_____

_____

_____

_____

Consider celebrating the sacrament of reconciliation. Make an appointment with one of your parish priests or attend a reconciliation service. Confess what you've found lurking in your inner garbage can and ask for forgiveness—not for being angry but for the sin of nursing your anger, for keeping a score of wrongs, and for being emotionally dishonest.

God Can Forgive You and Your Enemy

After you receive absolution for your sin, ask God to forgive the person who hurt you. That's right! Even before you try forgiving someone, ask God to wipe your enemy's slate clean. You may not be ready to let go of your anger, but God is ready to begin the restoration process. As you bring your anger before God in simple sorrow, you open yourself to God's power to free you from the burden of forgiving when you don't think you're ready.

Then and only then are you ready to ask God to help you forgive. If you don't feel any rush of peace or joy, don't worry; trust God to begin a work in you that only divine love can initiate.

Don't keep checking to see whether you've let go of your

anger; instead, every time you think of that person or feel your anger boiling up inside you, think, *Thank God this is being taken care of. I don't have to work on it right now. I only have to have faith that Christ is sovereign over my inner life.* Record the date you begin this process.

Date _____

If you don't feel this process has released you from unforgiveness, don't worry about that either; remind yourself that God is helping you. Pray, "Lord, I forgive; help my unforgiveness."

Living Saints

If you can't think of a single person you don't love unconditionally, you are a living saint or you're very good at denying your feelings.

Get away from others for a while: go on retreat, take a long hike in the woods, or spend a day beside the ocean. Get away for a few days, even a few hours, and pray intensely. Ask God to show you anyone you haven't forgiven: your third-grade playmate, a piano teacher who humiliated you, the unreasonable boss on your first job, or the spouse who shows off by making you the butt of jokes.

Ask God to show you the lining of your heart: is it upholstered in love, or are you harboring old anger behind black curtains? Enter into deep, silent prayer and give yourself permission to see the truth. Then journal your experience in the pages provided or in your notebook.

Journal

_____

_____

_____

_____

_____

_____

_____

_____

_____

_____

_____

_____

_____

_____

_____

_____

_____

_____

2.
"Whom Should I Pray For?"

"To you who hear I say, love your enemies, do good to those who hate you, bless those who curse you, pray for those who mistreat you."

Luke 6:27-28

Prayer

God, let me be open in my heart and mind, ready to learn as you teach me new ways to pray.

Amen

The Teaching

We often pray for our friends. Sometimes we pray for our enemies, asking God to change their hearts or teach them wisdom. But Jesus asks us for a deeper commitment to prayer, for a more radical obedience of his commandment to pray for our enemies.

In early childhood, most of us learned to intercede for others: "God bless Mommy and Daddy and Grandma and Uncle Joe..." We continue in that pattern of prayer in adulthood: we ask God's blessings on our loved ones, the pope, the Church, the nation's leaders, crops and farmers, friends who are sick and dying, our favorite politicians, and on those who minister as pastors, physicians, teachers, and nurses. We beseech God to be merciful to our spouse and children, to deliver hostages and those who are persecuted, and to shower blessings on those who deserve them.

These are good, solid prayers. But they're not all Jesus asks us to do. Scripture offers us a picture in which the intercessor prays for his or her enemies and for those who have sinned against them and against God.

The Old Testament

In spite of his own anger about the golden calf, Moses implored God to forgive the people of Israel. Because Moses prayed, God did forgive them (Exodus 32:1-20).

Job prayed for his three comforters who had upbraided him in his deepest distress. Because Job prayed, God forgave the unrighteous men (Job 42:7-9).

God told Hosea to take back, forgive, and love his adulterous wife. Then God held up this tender treatment as an example of forgiveness toward adulterous Israel (Hosea 1–3).

The prophet Isaiah foretold that the Messiah would make "intercession for the transgressors" (Isaiah 53:12; NRSV).

To gain a deeper understanding of these Scriptures, answer the following questions referring to the references noted above.

What did God offer Moses?

_____

Why, do you think, did Moses refuse?

_____

_____

_____

How did God show acceptance of Moses' intercession?

_____

What did God say to Job's comforters?

_____

Was their sacrifice significant? Why?

_____

What does Hosea's story tell us?

_____

Why did God let the faithless of Israel be saved?

_____

What are the outstanding qualities of the prophesied Savior in Isaiah 53?

_____

The Old Testament offers a record of Israel's faithlessness and God's redemption. Even though they had seen miracles and had eaten manna every day for forty years, the children of Israel disbelieved and disobeyed their God. They refused to enter the promised land. After they did come into Canaan, they rejected God as sovereign and asked for kings, who then set up pagan worship centers. They disobeyed God's edicts to help the poor. Finally, they were exiled. But God forgave them over and over, finally sending Jesus Christ to redeem the world.

The New Testament

The New Testament offers strong instructions about and examples of forgiveness.

Read Luke 6:27-36. Jesus tells us to _____ our enemies, _____ to those who hate us, _____ those who curse us, and to _____ for those who mistreat us. Jesus reminds us to _____ to our enemies without expecting repayment.

Read John 13:2-5. Knowing Judas Iscariot would soon betray him, Jesus nevertheless _____ Judas' _____.

Read Luke 22:50-51. Jesus _____ the _____ of the high priest's servant.

Read Luke 23:34-41. Jesus _____ for the men who crucified him, asking God to _____ them. He took a criminal, a convicted thief, to _____.

Read John 20:23. After the Resurrection, Jesus' first charge to his disciples concerned the _____ of sins.

Read Acts 7:60. The Church's first martyr, Saint Stephen, prayed that those who stoned him to death _____.

The ultimate example of intercession for sinners is, of course, the atoning work of our Lord, Jesus Christ. Though blameless in every way, he took on himself the sins of the world—including our own—thus gaining eternal life for all who follow him.

After you read the New Testament examples above, meditate on the following questions:

- Do I really want to love and obey Jesus Christ?
- Am I as forgiving as he asks me to be?
- Who do I need to pray for?

Praying for Your Enemies

Someone has said, "Think of the person you like the least. That's how much you really love God."

This sentence isn't meant to make us feel guilty; it's meant to help us see how much we need to grow. Prayer—especially praying for others—is the richest form of growth.

Whom should you pray for? your friends and loved ones? Of course. But Jesus reminds us that even sinners and tax collectors can love their families and friends. Furthermore, your friends and loved ones don't need your prayers nearly as much as those who reject Jesus, who hurt others, who lead the world to war, who hate you or hate the Church. These people desperately need to feel the power of God's love.

- Pray for difficult in-laws and for the sibling you've always resented. Pray for parents who raised you wrong.
- Pray for world leaders: our president, governors, and senators, especially those whose politics don't agree with yours. Pray for the governments of foreign states.
- Pray for all Christian denominations, blessing all who minister in the name of Jesus. Pray for Buddhists, Muslims, Zoroastrians, Hindus, and Jews. Pray for cult members, for writers and speakers and teachers who criticize Catholics, and for those who scoff at Christianity. Pray for all those who are persecuted for their beliefs.
- Pray for terrorists, rapists, abortionists, adulterers, pornographers, child molesters, murderers, spouse-beaters, polluters of our environment, thieves, liars, loan sharks, prostitutes, and members of organized crime.

There's nothing in the Bible that suggests we can even ask these people to reform. Instead of prayers for changed behavior, your prayers must be prayers of blessing.

Blessing List

Begin by praying for your enemies on a reasonable scale with specific categories and specific names.

List three people who upset your personal life in some way: family members, neighbors, business associates, the pastor, the choir director, a teacher, or other persons who irritate or anger you or of whom you deeply disapprove.

1. _____

2. _____

3. _____

Now, list three more people who you think are dangerous to the Church or to the world: dictators, generals, authors, or public figures. Make these specific people; don't just pray for these kinds of people in general. Look through your newspaper or listen to a news broadcast and pick particular individuals.

1. _____

2. _____

3. _____

Finally, list three people who are an insult and danger to society: rapists, murderers, pornographers. Make these specific people; don't just pray for murderers in general. Look through your newspaper or listen to a news broadcast and pick particular individuals.

1. _____

2. _____

3. _____

Prayer is a learning experience as well as a spiritual exercise. As you grow in Christ, you'll be able to add more names to your list of "enemy intercessions."

Promise God that you will pray for these nine people every single day for the next three months. In your prayer, do not advise God to change them. Simply pray for God to bless them.

All Things Are Possible With God

Who can pray with love for a murderer, a child molester, or a parent who has always been abusive?

Nobody. And a camel can't go through a needle's eye. You *can't* pray for your enemies until you ask God for strength and inspiration. Then the system changes: your prayer loses rancor. In the name of Jesus, you are able to forgive all your enemies—and God's enemies—as you pray, "God bless the terrorists (or pro-choice advocates or mean landlords or drug peddlers)."

My friend Leta was assaulted while walking home from work at sundown. Despite her screams, the attacker covered her mouth, threw her onto the lawn behind the hedge, and raped her. He then fled into the dark. Eventually, people heard her screams and came to her aid. But it was too late. Leta had been attacked in mind, body, and emotions; she wanted to die.

Leta's pastor, as well as personnel from the local rape crisis center, tried to help her immediate hurt and rage. But Leta was emotionally damaged, almost defeated. She quit her job, broke her engagement to the man she loved, and went back to her hometown. For months, she hid in the bedroom of her parents' home, refusing to see her fiancé or old friends. Finally, expecting to hear comforting words, Leta allowed a nun from her home parish to visit her. She was shocked to hear Sister Patricia say, "Leta, I want you to bless that man!"

Leta ordered the nun to leave and retreated to her room. Sister Patricia, however, left behind a handwritten reference to Luke 6.

Although Leta read the note and threw it away, she couldn't get the nun's voice out of her head. Again and again, she heard the command, "Bless that man!"

After several sleepless nights and difficult days, Leta sat on the edge of her bed with her fists clenched. She whispered, "God bless the man that raped me...."

Leta didn't feel like blessing her attacker, but in the spirit of obedience, she said the words. At dinner that night, she noticed her appetite was better than it had been for months. Connecting that slight improvement to her prayer, she uttered another prayer of blessing for her attacker. Within a few days, Leta called Sister Patricia and made an appointment to see her. It was the first time Leta had been out of the house in three weeks.

When the rapist was captured and brought to trial for several counts of rape, Leta testified against him. Rather than demanding revenge, however, Leta asked the judge to send the man where he would get help, so he could redeem his life. To her rapist, Leta said, "I will pray for you."

Today, Leta is married to her longtime sweetheart and works at a women's counseling center, where she is known as "Bless-'em-all Leta." The man who raped her is in a prison sex-offender program. Leta prays for him every day.

More than one life was redeemed in this process: Leta's, her rapist's, her distraught parents', and her fiancé's. "One word changed me from an angry, depressed victim into a victorious woman of God," Leta says. "The word was *bless.*"

Prayer: The People Changer

Bumper stickers and posters declare, "Prayer changes things." The truth is, prayer changes people. Anytime you communicate with God, you are changed. When you pray prayers of forgiveness and blessing, you become a new creation, just as Leta did.

For the next three months, pray for the nine people you listed on page 24. If you are creative and alert and listen to God in your heart, I offer this guarantee: if you aren't satisfied at the end of this period, you can go back to being the person you were before you started.

Journal

_____

_____

_____

_____

_____

_____

_____

_____

_____

_____

_____

_____

_____

_____

_____

_____

_____

_____

_____

_____

3.
How to Bless When Forgiving Is Hard

"...just before you came...I blessed him. Now he must remain blessed!"

Genesis 27:33

Prayer

O God, you have blessed us since our creation. Grant me the wisdom and strength to bless others, especially those who have hurt me.

Amen

The Teaching

The act of blessing has real power, yet requires only a will to obey Jesus combined with a small effort on our part.

In the movie *The Dollmaker,* the heroine whispers through the wall to her sobbing neighbor, "The Lord bless thee and keep thee, the Lord make his face to shine upon thee and be gracious unto thee. The Lord lift up his countenance upon thee and give thee peace."

That woman who carved dolls wasn't just murmuring the biblical equivalent of "Have a good day." She was offering the reality of God's presence, repeating the very words God gave to the first high priest, Aaron, for blessing the people of Israel.

Ancient Blessings

Throughout the Scriptures, we see that the act of blessing has an important ritualistic role; it is more than a polite exchange. Read through the Scriptures below and fill in the blanks.

Read Genesis 27:1-29. To receive his father's blessing, the final word, as it were, Jacob disguises himself as his _____. When Isaac discovers that Jacob has tricked him into giving his blessing, Isaac nevertheless says, "I _____ him and therefore he must remain _____."

Read Genesis 32:23-31. When Jacob wrestled with God, he says, "I will not let you go until you _____ me," placing himself in peril of destruction to receive his Visitor's blessing.

Read Genesis 48:8-20. Although Joseph is virtual ruler of all Egypt, he rushes his sons to their aged grandfather, _____, also called _____, for a blessing.

Throughout the ancient Hebrew Scriptures, we read about fathers and mothers blessing their children, prophets blessing kings, and devout men and women praying for God to bless them.

The blessing of a father on his son was tantamount to appointing him his heir and executor; the blessing could not be undone. Maybe that's why Jacob insisted that his "wrestling partner" give him a blessing—so that later, God could not withdraw his favor.

The Word of the Lord

Blessing has divine power attached to it. Little wonder, then, that we sometimes begin the sacrament of reconciliation by asking for a blessing and linger at Mass until the blessing of the Trinity is pronounced. The sacraments of baptism and marriage contain this same kind of blessing. When we say to one another "God bless you," we utter the most powerful words in the universe.

We say these words to our friends, especially as they embark on new ventures, when they're sick, or when they're grieving; to our children and relatives at their birthday parties and weddings; to our friends at church, as we shake hands and go home. But what about our enemies?

We've already seen that Christ expects us to bless those who curse us, returning good prayers for ugly words. But some of us, for deeply personal reasons, may find it hard to start this process.

Identification

In the previous two chapters, you identified nine people as "enemies." In the following space, write the names of those people:

_____

_____

_____

_____

_____

_____

_____

_____

_____

As you grow in grace, you'll continue to add to the list of people God wants you to pray for. You'll keep digging through any emotional garbage piles or hiding places inside you.

Now, ask God to reveal to you anyone whose feelings you may have hurt.

_____

_____

_____

Look back over your life. Are you avoiding or blaming people for something you did that hurt them? Are you blaming circumstances for something? Have you attached these circumstances to someone like a parent, teacher, boss, spouse, or friend who created or caused events that kept you from success or love or happiness? List the people or situations you've been blaming for your own shortcomings.

_____

_____

_____

If you're not quite ready to go beyond your original list of nine, or if you can't think of anyone else, ask God to continue to open your heart further. As new names come to mind, list them. These names, along with the nine people you promised to pray for, and the ones above, will be your Blessing List.

_____

_____

_____

As names continue to come to you, add them to the journal pages at the end of this chapter or list them in your notebook.

Blessing When Forgiving Is Hard

"I still haven't forgiven my husband for lying to me about borrowing money from his mother," admits Elise. "I've tried, and I've prayed, but I can't."

Elise—and you—needn't concentrate on forgiveness just yet. Elise—and you—have to move toward forgiveness. First, write the name(s) of anyone you feel you absolutely cannot forgive.

_____

_____

Now pray, "God, I want to forgive _____, and I ask you to bless them." Then turn your awareness toward blessing.

You never have to enjoy the company of the persons you're praying for (although eventually you may). You don't have to approve of what they've done or are doing. You don't even have to work at being more loving. For now, just bless them.

How? Open your mouth and say, "God, please bless _____ _____ today. Amen." It's that simple—and that profound.

Don't worry about feeling forgiving, loving, or caring. Christianity isn't a religion of feelings or sensory experiences; Christianity is a Person, the person of Jesus Christ, who redeems us. He asks us to bless our enemies—not when we feel like it, when forgiveness is completed, or when we've made up with the person. Jesus asks us to bless these people now; Christianity is always *now*.

Speaking the Word

The spoken word is powerful. That's why our responses at Mass and corporate prayers, like novenas and rosaries, are spoken aloud. As you prepare to pray for your enemies, focus on finding ways and times to do it out loud. You may have to hide in the bathroom and mutter your blessings toward the shower curtain. You may have to sing them as you push your basket through the grocery store. If you drive to and from work alone, you can pray in full voice. Whenever and wherever you pray, loudly ask God's blessings on your enemies. Say, "God, please bless _____ today." Let yourself hear your own words.

Make a list of times and places you will commit to blessing the people on your list.

_____

_____

Write the prayer you're going to say about each person on your list.

_____

_____

_____

_____

_____

_____

Why is it important to verbalize your blessing? For insight, read Matthew 15:11. Jesus said, "It is not what enters one's mouth that defiles that person; but what _____ _____ of the mouth is what defiles one." The converse is also true; the good words we speak can actually purify us and make us holier. A psychologist would call this "repeated auditory reinforcement" because what we hear ourselves saying over and over has a profound effect on the brain.

What prayers have you said aloud all your life, at Mass or in other circumstances?

_____

_____

_____

You probably could say these prayers in your sleep. They're part of you. In the same manner, your prayers of blessing have to become a part of you. When you ask God to bless people, you aren't asking a faraway God to do some nice thing to an equally faraway enemy. You're inviting the Holy Spirit to create a profound change in you, a change that will make you stronger and holier, a change that will connect you through your will and words to another person. Frequently verbalizing your prayer allows the prayer to become as familiar as the ones you memorized long ago and remember today.

Extend each blessing individually, ending each with "Amen." Don't just say, "God, please bless John and Mother and Cynthia and the man at the bank and my fourth-grade teacher." You need more individual focus. You need to say and hear all the words for each person. You're pleading with God. Your "Amen," meaning "truly" in Greek and "so be it" in Hebrew, adds your vocal intention that this prayer be carried out.

"Wait," you say. "That could take hours every day." Actually, to say a blessing for nine people takes less than a minute. You can bless thirty people in about three minutes or less: such a brief amount of time that can begin a life change.

Remember: don't pause to concentrate on forgiving anyone during your prayer. Forgiveness is part of the fruit of the prayer of blessing. Both your mouth and your mind are changed by this process.

The Epistle of James is startlingly straightforward about the power of blessing. Read 3:5-12. Specifically note what James says about blessings and curses (v. 10-11): "From the same mouth come _____ and _____. This need not be so, my brothers. Does a spring gush forth from the same opening both _____ and _____ water?"

When you bless your enemies again and again, eventually your "spring" has a harder time saying ugly words about anyone. In fact, you may find yourself a lot closer to genuine forgiveness than ever before.

Praying the Hardest Prayers of All

Undoubtedly, there are people or groups that fill you with tremendous rage. Maybe you feel especially angry toward a parent or stepparent who abused or molested you. Perhaps you hold a sharp contempt for the people who run the abortion clinic up the street. Maybe your hatred centers on a rapist or burglar who has caused tremendous suffering for you, your family, or some loved ones. If you are to be a whole person, these people merit your prayer. Remember, we are not focusing on forgiveness at this point; we are focusing on blessing.

You may actually choke the first time you stammer, "God, please bless _____. Amen." In fact, your pain may make you feel dizzy. Don't dwell on the pain; concentrate on the blessing. To let you know that your anger is literally eating you up, stomach acid may well up in your esophagus as you say the words. Offer that anger to God; let God redeem it—and move on to the next person on your list. There will be time to work on your pain—when you're able. In the meantime, the prayer of blessing does not interfere with any kind of therapy you may be undergoing. (An additional word of caution is in order: if someone has left you with serious emotional problems that make the prayer of blessing impossible for you, get a mental-health professional to help you before taking this step.)

Don't get stuck on that hardest-to-forgive person. Don't review what that person has done to you or others. Just pray for the person and go on. No matter how much hurt or fury you hold toward that person, you can make your mouth say the words of blessing, even if your fists are clenched while you do so.

Don't save that person for last; you may find excuses for skipping him or her indefinitely. In fact, I put this person at the top of my list. Once I get past the most difficult name, I can continue praying for those who—somehow—I've begun to feel a little friendlier toward.

Journal

_____

_____

_____

_____

_____

_____

_____

_____

_____

_____

_____

_____

_____

_____

_____

_____

_____

_____

_____

_____

_____

4.

Painkiller Emotions

*The intention in the human heart is like water far below
    the surface,
    but the [person] of intelligence draws it forth.*

Proverbs 20:5

Prayer

O God, you are the balm for all suffering. Help me
look deep within myself, that I may give up anger and
sorrow and strive for wholeness.

Amen

The Teaching

Anger and resentment can obscure the pain you
experience in relationships. Only when you face that
pain are you able to forgive.

Now that you've blessed your enemies for a while, it's time to
check your emotional pulse, just as you would check your pulse
throughout an exercise workout.

Do I have any uncomfortable leftover feelings toward the
people I've been blessing and forgiving? Describe those feelings.

_____

_____

_____

_____

Do I still "brace myself" when I have to meet one of those people? Am I afraid there will be a scene? Describe your thoughts and feelings.

_____

_____

_____

Do I still have occasional blowups with a person I think I've forgiven? Do I come away from the person feeling upset? Describe how you feel afterward and where you feel it physically.

_____

_____

_____

_____

A Brief History of Resentment

Irene was a forgiving person. When someone injured her, she was quick to ask God to help her forgive. She never tried to "get even" with her older sister, for example, who verbally abused her all her life. Although Irene said that she had forgiven her sister, however, she knew some ancient anger was still active.

"O God, I've been forgiving my sister over and over for her verbal abuse," Irene prayed. "Every time I see her, she hurts me again and I forgive her again. But there's always something left behind—a little knot in my stomach."

"Yes," God seemed to answer in Irene's mind,"it's resentment: a little knot of leftover anger. You're using it as an anesthetic."

Searching for Painkillers

What do the words *anesthetic* and *anesthesia* mean to you?

anesthetic _____

anesthesia _____

Check your dictionary to see if there are any other meanings you didn't know about. Make note of them here.

_____

_____

Now, think back through your own medical history. In the chart below, list the over-the-counter painkillers you've used (such as aspirin, Tylenol, or Ben-Gay) and the kind of pain you used them for (such as headache, a twisted leg muscle, or a sore back).

Painkiller	Kind of Pain
_____	_____
_____	_____
_____	_____
_____	_____

If you need more space, use the journal pages at the end of this chapter.

Next, list the names of medicines a dentist or doctor has given you and the pain you took them for (such as Novocaine for the pain of dental work or codeine for a sprained ankle).

Painkiller   **Kind of Pain**

_____   _____

_____   _____

_____   _____

_____   _____

Try to remember some pain that returned after the painkiller wore off. Your headaches might have lasted longer than the aspirin; your broken leg might have kept throbbing despite codeine or Demerol. Make note of these experiences.

_____

_____

Have you ever had a general anesthesia, the kind that makes you drowsy (like sodium pentothal or laughing gas for dental work) or that numbs most of your body (like a spinal anesthesia for back surgery or a hysterectomy)? List those experiences.

Anesthetic   **Reason Used**

_____   _____

_____   _____

_____   _____

When these anesthetics wore off were you out of pain or did you ask for other painkillers?

Resentment as Painkiller

It's unlikely that the painkillers or anesthetics you've taken were permanent. The pain probably returned to some degree. You had to keep taking the medicine until the condition healed.

Here's a modern proverb to remember: "Those who use anger or resentment to cover up pain will have the pain again when they get rid of anger." The converse is true as well: "Accessing old pain will dissipate the resentment you've employed to cover it up."

Irene had to bypass her "anesthetic" and allow herself to feel the pain she had blocked for years. She didn't have just one incident to relive; she had a whole lifetime of being manipulated and verbally abused by her sister.

She decided to reexperience all the memories of pain she had buried. Through intense prayer, journaling, and talking to her confessor and a trusted friend, Irene began to deliberately dredge up memory after memory. This time, however, she did not quickly say, "I forgive my sister"; she did not block the hurt her memories produced. Instead, Irene allowed herself to feel the pain. Always, her reaction to the pain was tears.

"I cried all that Lent," Irene recalls. "I cried in the morning, I cried every evening, remembering one incident after another. Sometimes I cried on my coffee breaks at work. I cried driving home. But by Easter morning, I was healed."

Irene's pain had been redemptive. She was no longer full of unresolved resentment toward her sister—or toward anyone else for that matter. By allowing herself to be hurt, she became stronger, not weaker. "And finally forgave my sister for the first time," she confesses.

The Steps Before Forgiving

Before starting to talk seriously about forgiving those enemies, friends, or family members who are wrecking your peace, do your homework. Dig around in your soul for painkiller emotions like anger or resentment, or behaviors like coldness, screaming, or slamming things around. You have used these emotions and behaviors to anesthetize yourself, to keep the other person from "winning."

When you first started the journey of blessing your enemies, you set pain and anger aside while you prayed. You've grown enough now to think about your deepest feelings. If you're chronically angry and don't know why, you may need professional assistance in uncovering the roots of your rage. If you were severely abused as a child or young person, do not attempt to relive your problem without a mental-health professional.

But if, like Irene, you've tried to forgive someone and still have lingering resentment, the following exercises will help you turn off the anesthetic and help you start living with peace.

Perhaps your high school English teacher picked on you, humiliating you in front of the entire class. When you knocked yourself out to turn in a perfect report, she took you to the principal and accused you of cheating.

That teacher is now a tiny old lady who comes to your parish church. When you look at her, you don't see a frail old woman; you see the teacher who made your life miserable. Every time you see her, the old anger is evident.

Maybe your father was demanding and critical. No matter how hard you tried to please him, he found a flaw in what you did. Maybe he continues to do that today, and you keep forgiving him—and resenting him.

Have you been hurt by someone you trusted? betrayed at work by your closest ally? Has your fiancée fallen for another person? Has your spouse betrayed a confidence?

Whatever it is, if your feelings of anger are stronger than your feelings of pain, you may be "anesthetizing."

The Example of Jesus

"Suppose I do have buried pain, why should I dig up old hurts? Life is hard enough." That's a common response. Why, indeed, would anyone want to dig up old suffering and endure it again? Why? To become a whole person, alive in Christ.

Jesus never denied his pain. When he was in the wilderness, tempted by Satan, he was desperately hungry; but what did he say when the devil told him to turn stones into bread? (See Matthew 4:1-11.)

_____

_____

When Jesus was flogged and crowned with thorns before his crucifixion, did he get even? No. As nails were pound into his hands and feet, what did Jesus say? (See Luke 23:34.)

_____

When he was crucified and his executioners offered him a painkiller—wine drugged with myrrh to anesthetize his pain—what did Jesus do? (See Mark 15:23.)

_____

_____

Did Jesus ever accuse anyone or ask God to destroy his enemies?

_____

We sometimes look at Jesus through his Resurrection and Ascension and forget that he is also the quintessential man. If we want to be whole, strong people, we have an example. Jesus never denied the truth, In fact, he said that the truth would set us _____!

Use the following steps to move toward self-understanding and personal truth.

1. Examine your soul and find your pain. Admit to yourself that the resentment that kills pain is present in you, even if it isn't active anger. Ask God to forgive you. Ask God to forgive the person who hurt you, even though you're not ready to forgive him or her. Who caused the pain in your memory?

_____

What feelings or behaviors are your anesthetic(s)?

_____

_____

_____

_____

2. Through journaling and talking with a trusted friend or confessor, return to the incident(s) that you've been angry about. You may have a list of hurts a mile long; you may have only a few. List them in your journal, talk them out, or both. If your memory is hazy, ask God to show you the whole picture. Try to relive the event: let your sister scream at you; let your boss shake his finger in your face; see your father express his disapproval and coldly walk away.

Record the date when you begin this process.

Date _____

3. Now, before anger rushes in to fill the space, allow your pain to emerge. It's there. Nobody can go through these experiences without getting hurt. The trouble is, you may have learned to switch off pain before you even feel it.

Act out your pain—not your anger. Unclench your fists, put your angry chin down, bow your head, and feel the pain. Where is it? Is it tightening your throat or stiffening your limbs? Let go. Cry, wail, sniffle, shout, and sob. Say the words that express pain. Say, "It hurts! It makes me ache! I feel like throwing myself on the floor." If you're able, go ahead and throw yourself on the floor or the bed and sob it out.

Do this as many times as necessary. Maybe you need to do it once or, like Irene, maybe you need to cry your way through Lent (or whatever season you're in). Don't stop until you're empty. Write your feelings here.

_____

_____

_____

_____

_____

_____

_____

_____

_____

_____

_____

Record the date when you begin this process.

Date _____

4. *Comfort yourself.* Notice I did not say, "Justify yourself." Don't tell yourself that you were right and the other person had no business treating you that way. That's how you worked up that anesthetic anger to start with! Instead, talk to the person inside yourself who has suffered; talk to that person just like you'd talk to a hurt child. "It's okay, honey. You're starting to feel better now...I know you were really hurt. You felt terrible, didn't you." Say whatever kind words come to mind. Do you feel silly? Do it anyway. That wounded child or betrayed man or woman inside you needs to hear some caring words.

Make note of the words that help you most.

_____

_____

_____

Record the date.

Date _____

5. *Repeat until healed.* You'll know when you're healed. The people around you will know; they'll comment about how rested you look, how calm you seem to be. Mainly, you'll notice a lessening and eventual vanishing of that burning sensation in your chest or the ache between your eyes that would settle in every time you thought of the person who hurt you. At that time, and only then, are you ready to begin the forgiveness process.

Journal

_____

_____

_____

_____

_____

_____

_____

_____

_____

_____

_____

_____

_____

_____

_____

_____

_____

_____

5.

What Forgiving Is—And Isn't

And when he had said this, he breathed on them and said to them,
"Receive the holy Spirit. Whose sins you forgive are forgiven
them, and whose sins you retain are retained."

John 20:22-23

Prayer

O God, you have forgiven my sins and redeemed me
through the blood of Jesus Christ. Help me have
mercy and forgive in that same way.

Amen

The Teaching

We're ready to talk about forgiveness. The grace to
forgive is given by God not as a chore but as a
blessing. Forgiveness is more than understanding or
letting it go; it's a dynamic system that connects you
and others to Christ.

Peter was showing off. "Shall I forgive my brother seven
times?" he asked Jesus. *Look how well I know the Law,* he
thought. *Look how merciful I am. I'm willing to forgive my
brother—that is, another Jewish person—over and over again,
even up to seven times!* (See Matthew 18:21.)

But Jesus knocked Peter off his self-assured high horse very quickly. "No, Peter. Forgive your brother seventy times seven!" (See Matthew 18:22.)

That doesn't mean that you keep a careful record to make sure you remit someone's sins exactly 490 times. Rather, it means forgiving without counting at all.

But why? Why should we continue to forgive someone who has hurt us over and over again?

Forgiveness and Health

Forgiveness certainly isn't just a rule God made out of whimsy. It isn't something that makes God feel better. Forgiving our enemies does a number of things, one of which is to make us feel more alive, more joyful.

Name one person you enjoy being with, someone who adds to your life. What emotion do you feel with regard to this person? joy? security? warmth?

Name _____

Emotion _____

Now, name one person you have not been able to forgive. This may be a difficult person from one of your lists. What emotion do you feel when you think about this person? It may be rage or hurt; it may be guilt.

Name _____

Emotion _____

Who else do you find difficult to forgive? This might include someone you love—a spouse or child or parent—who did something (or continues to do something) that you find painful.

Do you have a major "enemy," someone who ruined your business or hurt you or someone you love.

In the space provided below, write the names of these people on the left and the emotions connected with that person on the right. Be honest about your emotions. (This is not a test; you will not be graded.)

Name	**Emotion**
_____	_____
_____	_____
_____	_____
_____	_____
_____	_____
_____	_____

If you need more space, use a separate sheet of paper. You'll refer to this list later, so keep it inside these pages.

Before we talk about forgiving these people, review your emotions connected with each of them. Are they feelings you enjoy? Are they the emotions you feel on a spring afternoon when the fruit trees have burst into clouds of blossom and the warm sun soaks the winter out of your bones? Probably not. Your emotions probably remind you of walking in sleet-laden gusts of wind or feeling exhausted on a day when the temperature soars over ninety degrees. Negative emotions do more than make you feel unhappy; negative emotions affect you physically.

Concentrate on one of the people you listed above and allow your emotions to take over. Feel all the anger or pain that person's presence can bring you. Notice where you feel these emotions. Does a tight band cut across your chest? Do you experience a headache, a rush of indigestion, or a tightening of the muscles between your shoulder blades? What areas of your body are involved with the emotion toward anyone you haven't forgiven?

_____

_____

_____

_____

Now, let's try an experiment. Imagine yourself forgiving that person. In your mind, see the person coming toward you. Instead of bracing yourself for a confrontation or walking away, run toward that person; embrace that person. Whisper, "_____ , I forgive you, and God forgives you." If, in your imagination, the person tries to explain or apologize, say, "No, you don't have to be sorry. I have forgiven you, and we'll never speak of it again."

How did you feel as you tried that exercise? Did you feel a release of tightness in your chest? Did your arms and legs relax?

_____

_____

_____

_____

It's healthier to forgive others than to let the thought of them cause your heart to pound, your breathing to speed up, and/or your vision to blur. Some people experience rashes, hives, and other blemishes on the surface of their skin as a result of harbored anger. Others hold unforgiveness within until they develop heart problems or permanent breathing difficulties. Forgiving is a healthy lifestyle.

The Tie That Binds

Beyond the benefit of being a healthier person, there is another benefit to forgiving others, one more mysterious.

Jesus gave Peter the keys of the kingdom of heaven and made Peter the rock on which he builds his Church. In Matthew 16:19, Jesus tells Peter, "Whatever you _____ on earth shall be _____ in heaven, and whatever you loose on earth shall be loosed in heaven."

After the Resurrection, Jesus again mentions the importance and power of forgiveness. In John 20:22-23, Jesus breathes on his disciples and says, "Receive the holy Spirit. Whose sins you _____ are forgiven them, and whose sins you _____ are retained."

Jesus says these words first to Peter, later to his disciples, and ultimately to all of us. We don't know what "binding" sins means. Perhaps Jesus is talking about the opposite of forgiveness, a binding that affects relationship with God. Suppose you had the power to keep a person out of God's grace forever—because you "bound" their sins in your unforgiveness!

"Forgive sins" is Jesus' first charge to the Church. All of us who try to follow the example of the first Christians must consider the dynamic power of our forgiveness.

Forgive Us Our Trespasses

You may be thinking, *I don't care if I do bind over John* (or Letitia or Uncle Henry) *for his sins. I don't care if he goes straight to hell!* Your feelings are understandable. But God has provided a reminder for such situations: the Our Father. Write the Our Father on the lines below.

_____

_____

_____

_____

_____

_____

_____

_____

_____

_____

When you pray the Our Father, how do you ask our Father in heaven to forgive your trespasses (or sins or wrongs, if you prefer the modern versions)?

As we _____

_____

_____

Read Matthew 6:9-15. What will your heavenly Father do if you forgive the sins of others?

_____

_____

What if you do not forgive the sins of others?

_____

_____

_____

Look over the list of people you can't forgive. You've been praying for God to bless your enemies. It's now time to think about forgiving them. Sound impossible? Wait! Don't give up!

Is there really anybody whose sins you won't forgive, thus bringing God's unforgiveness on yourself? Who can't or won't you forgive?

_____   _____

_____   _____

_____   _____

_____   _____

What did each of these persons do to earn your unforgiveness?

Person   **Act**

_____   _____

_____   _____

_____   _____

If you find that you absolutely cannot forgive these people, ask God to forgive them. Say the following prayer aloud, inserting the person's name and their action that blocks your forgiveness.

O God, I confess that I hold unforgiveness against _____. I ask, however, that you forgive him/her for _____

_____

_____.

I ask that you assist me by your grace in learning to forgive him/her. In the name of our Lord, Jesus Christ. Amen.

Repeat this prayer every day until you discover that God has softened your heart and has made you able to forgive.

What Forgiving Is Not

Have you ever said, "I forgive you—but..."?

Forgiveness doesn't mean reminding people of what they did to upset you; forgiveness doesn't mean adding instructions for future behavior. "I forgive you, but I hope you'll be more careful" is not the model of remission of sin that God gave us. When Jesus tells the woman accused of adultery to go and sin no more, his intention is to caution the woman against returning to the madness that had brought her to that moment in the first place. He does not mean to remind her of her offense.

"I can forgive John for being so rude , because I know he was having difficulty on his job." " Mom was terribly ill when I was a child, so I can forgive her for neglecting me." These are not examples of forgiveness; they are examples of understanding. You understand that John was in trouble at work; you understand your mother was very ill for many years.

True forgiveness, however, exists with or without understanding. When God forgives your sins, it isn't because of some elaborate explanation you cook up. God forgives because God loves. In fact, read the story of the Prodigal Son (Luke 15:11-24). Respond to the following statements by circling a, b, or c—whichever accurately completes the sentence. See how God forgives even before you ask.

The son decides to go home because he is
   (a) sorry
   (b) worried about his family
   (c) alone and hungry

The son expects to be treated by his father like
   (a) an honored guest
   (b) a servant
   (c) a son of the household

But before the son gets to his old home, his father
   (a) runs ahead to greet him
   (b) goes in the house and locks the door
   (c) waits on the porch for an apology

When his father embraces and kisses him, the son
   (a) explains his behavior as a psychological reaction to
       childhood intimidation by his older brother
   (b) asks to be taken home as a son of the house
   (c) confesses his sins

The father
   (a) ignores his son's confession and calls for rich gifts
   (b) thinks over the boy's plea for mercy and decides to teach
       him a lesson by making him a servant for a while
   (c) refuses to let his son in the house

Then the father
   (a) shows his son to his new quarters in the servants' cabins
   (b) summons the police to take the wastrel to jail
   (c) calls for a celebration

The father walks along the road, perhaps hoping against hope
that his son will return. Jesus then says that when the son is still

a long way off, the father sees him and runs to him, to claim him as no longer lost.

This is the way God treats us. God watches for us when we're a long way off. Because we are forgiven so much, we have a perfect example of how we are to forgive others.

Four-Step Ritual of Forgiveness

Use these steps to forgive each person on your list from page 55.

1. Write a confession to God that you have held a grudge or otherwise failed to forgive a person. It's easy to forget that unforgiveness is a sin against God. You may be a wonderful Christian, with only this one tiny stain on an otherwise perfect life. But God holds you responsible for all your misdoings, including this one. If possible, take this confession with you when you celebrate the sacrament of reconciliation. Write your confession here.

_____

_____

_____

_____

Record the date.

Date _____

2. Confess that you can't forgive this person without God's help. Perhaps years may have passed since the person offended you; perhaps the hurt is so new that it's still too painful to look at. God is already running down the road, preparing to embrace you as a son or a daughter and calling for a celebration. Just say, "I'm sorry. Please, help me." You'll discover that forgiveness is a lot easier than you thought. Write your prayer to God.

_____

_____

_____

3. Ritualize your forgiveness. Put a clean cloth on a table or desk and place a lighted candle in the middle. Wash your hands as a reminder of your baptism into the family of God. Read aloud the confession of unforgiveness and the prayer you wrote asking for God's help (both above). Remaining quiet for a few moments, let God's love and help rest in your heart. Then say the Our Father slowly. Listen to the words. Put the candle out.

4. If possible, communicate with that person and tell him or her about your change of heart. This is probably the most difficult step—and the most necessary. God has given many signs that we are forgiven: most notably, the sight of Christ on the cross. You need to give your "enemy" some indication that you have forgiven him or her too. If speaking directly with the person is impossible or entirely too difficult, write a brief note saying something like "I've been mad at you for a long time, but God has helped me. Please accept my forgiveness and my apology for holding a grudge."

If the person is a neighbor, buy some fruit or flowers and deliver them in person. If the person is a relative, let the rest of the family know the fight is over and don't add any remarks about the person that could undo God's grace.

If you have not forgiven someone who is already dead, visit the grave and leave fresh flowers, write a note to the person's relatives, or make a donation for a Mass in his or her memory.

Hard? Yes, but not impossible. And here's another guarantee: if you don't like the way you feel after forgiving someone, you may return to your old way of hatred and anger.

Journal

6.

Words That Make You Sick

"I tell you, on the day of judgment people will render an account for every careless word they speak. By your words you will be acquitted, and by your words you will be condemned."

Matthew 12:36-37

Prayer

Your words, O God, are holy; not mine. Help me guard the door of my mouth, to find pleasure in kindness, not cruelty, and to discipline the words that I say to others.

Amen

The Teaching

Words are a matter of life and death. You have to use them carefully when speaking to others. Cruelty and sarcasm can actually affect the physical bodies of their victims.

Respond to the following true/false statements, and rate yourself according to the code provided.

Part I

1. T F I have a pretty clever tongue.
2. T F I'm the "fastest gun in the west" when it comes to crackling sarcasm.

3.   T   F   I like to use humor on religious solicitors or salespeople at my door or on the phone.

4.   T   F   Sarcasm is just one more harmless form of humor.

5.   T   F   I enjoy comedians who "put down" their wives or others. After all, it's in fun.

6.   T   F   Words aren't important; it's what I do that counts.

7.   T   F   People take jokes too personally; they should learn to be better sports.

8.   T   F   Some of the people closest to me (spouse, kids, parents, coworkers) are too sensitive.

Part II

1.   T   F   Someone in my childhood jeered at me, put down my efforts, or was sarcastic with me.

2.   T   F   Someone I know today jeers at me, puts down my efforts, or is sarcastic with me.

3.   T   F   I can never think of fast answers or quick put-downs.

4.   T   F   I prefer humor that doesn't hurt anyone—including me.

5.   T   F   I have a number of small health problems.

6.   T   F   I always take to heart what people say.

7.   T   F   Someone close to me thinks I'm too "sensitive."

8.   T   F   You can't excuse everything just because it's funny.

Code for Part I: If you have two or more "true" responses, you may be contributing to someone's illness.

Code for Part II: If you have two or more "true" responses, you are (or have been) verbally abused, and that abuse may be making you sick.

Sticks, Stones—and Sarcasm

Look up the word *sarcasm* in your dictionary. What definitions are given? If the definition includes the roots of the word, note that here as well.

_____

_____

_____

In its original Greek, *sarcastic* means "to rend [or tear apart] the flesh." The effects of sarcasm are, indeed, ripping and painful. For example, physical reactions to biting irony and sneering criticism may include speeded-up heart rates, raised blood pressure, or an increase in stomach acids that slosh into the esophagus and cause scarring. Some people react to verbal injury with rapid breathing that can cause alkalosis in the brain. Others unconsciously tense their muscles until the blood and lubrication supply to bone ends are cut off and joints start aching. Some people grind their teeth until they become victims of a dental condition called temporomandibular joint syndrome (TMJ).

No, not every case of TMJ or arthritis is psychogenic, a result of someone's sarcasm. But every time you speak with derision and contempt—even with the intention of being funny—you may tear someone's mind and body to pieces. You may actually make someone sick.

When you're the victim of constant "flesh-tearing," some of your aches and pains may actually be a result of trying to ignore an abuser.

Our language reveals a lot about words that can hurt. Listen to the phrases we use to describe what sarcasm and contempt do to our physical bodies:

"Her words *ripped me to pieces.*"

"The professor's remarks *nailed me to the wall.*"

"My sister *cut me to the quick.*"

"He *put the knife in and twisted it.*"

And what did Jesus have to say about sneering? "...if you insult a brother or sister, you will be liable to the council; and if you say, 'You fool,' you will be liable to the hell of fire" (Matthew 5:22, NRSV).

Proverbs 18:21 mentions the power of the tongue: "_____ and _____ are in the power of the tongue." Does that mean over your own life alone, or does it mean that your words can literally harm others?

Role Models

Television comedians use biting sarcasm. We may unconsciously imitate these sharp-tongued actors, consoling ourselves that this is "innocent teasing." But no joke that makes another person the butt of it, that embarrasses or pokes fun at any person, gender, group, race, or nationality, is funny.

Jesus never said, "Take my disciples. Please," even though those disciples were at times thick-headed and stumbling. Although the gospels are full of small jokes Jesus made, he never made jokes at the expense of others. He was filled with love. He let his yea be yea and his nay be nay. He confronted his enemies directly, not with sarcasm or left-handed remarks. Jesus is a far better role model than any television entertainer.

How to Change

Take stock of your life. Are you a victim of a sarcastic person? Does someone tease to the point of tears or tell you distasteful jokes that belittle others?

Are you the perpetrator of sarcasm? Do you make cracks at family members, coworkers, or ethnic groups?

You can change both kinds of behavior.

If you are the victim of constant sarcasm:

Confront your abuser. If necessary, ask a good friend to be present (but silent). Explain to the abusive person that his or her remarks bring you pain and that you want him or her to stop. Record the reaction the person has when you confront him or her. Record the date.

Reaction _____

_____

_____

Date _____

How did you feel when you confronted the person? happy? angry? paralyzed with fear?

_____

_____

_____

Do you think your confrontation did any good? Why or why not?

_____

_____

_____

Remove yourself from the situation if the person persists. Arrange to be too busy to talk in the office. Stay away from parties where the person might be. If you carpool, make new arrangements. If the person is a housemate, look for another rental. Even if you fail in these efforts, continue to look for opportunities to put distance between yourself and this person. What steps will you take to bring about these changes? Record the date you decided to make these changes.

Steps _____

_____

_____

_____

_____

_____

Date _____

How will your life be better as a result of these changes?

_____

_____

_____

How will these changes make life difficult for you?

_____

_____

_____

What alternatives can you try if these changes don't work?

_____

_____

_____

Face reality. If the person who hurts you is your spouse, parent, sibling, or boss, learn to manage your own reactions by blessing the person, forgiving him or her, and consciously releasing your resentment. Record the prayer you will offer for this person. Record the date you take this step.

Prayer   _____

_____

_____

_____

_____

_____

Date   _____

Insulate yourself. Jesus loves you enough to die for you. Write a thanksgiving for God's unconditional love.

_____

_____

_____

Copy this prayer on an index card and post it where you can see it every day: on your desk, refrigerator, nightstand, or mirror.

If you are a sarcastic person:

Confess your sin. Admit to God that your pattern of humor is cruel and dangerous to others' health, and that you need to change your behavior. If possible, confess this sin to a priest and listen to his counsel. Record the steps you will take to effect a change in your behavior. Record the date you make this change.

Steps _____

_____

_____

_____

_____

_____

Date _____

Apologize. Humbly admit to those you've hurt that sarcasm has been a source of sin in your life. Assure them that you will no longer be a source of pain to them. To whom will you apologize?

_____   _____

_____   _____

_____   _____

Ask for help. Suggest to your spouse, child, sibling, friend, coworker, or anyone who has been hurt by your sarcasm, that he or she give you a signal when you're "doing it again." This "signal" can be a word like *foul* or *ouch.* When you're given this signal, stop! Don't become argumentative and defensive. Stop! Think! Remember! You have promised God that you will change your behavior. What will your signal be?

_____

Seek inspiration. Every day for one month, read Matthew 5, 6, and 7. This discourse of Jesus summarizes the Christian model of love. If you can't finish all three chapters each day, read what you can and finish the reading the next day. Meditate on these

Scriptures until they're part of you. Record the dates you begin and end this month-long reading effort.

Beginning date _____

Ending date _____

Look for new role models. If your parents were sarcastic and biting in their treatment of you or each other, find others you can emulate. Otherwise, you risk repeating your parents' mistakes with your own spouse and kids. List those people you would like to model; include people you know personally as well as popular personalities.

People You Know	**Popular Personalities**
_____	_____
_____	_____
_____	_____
_____	_____

Again, refer to the Letter of James. The tongue is compared to a fire (3:6-12). "It exists among our members as a world of _____, defiling the whole body and setting the entire course of our lives on fire....No human being can tame the _____. It is a restless _____, full of deadly _____. With it we _____ the Lord and Father, and with it we _____ human beings who are made in the likeness of God. From the same mouth come _____ and _____." Somehow, cursing and blessings come out of the same mouth. But a fig tree can't produce olives (v. 12), so a person dedicated to Christ must control that fire-making tongue.

Journal

_____

_____

_____

_____

_____

_____

_____

_____

_____

_____

_____

_____

_____

_____

_____

_____

_____

_____

_____

7.
Rush to Judgment

"Stop judging, that you may not be judged. For as you judge, so will you be judged, and the measure with which you measure will be measured out to you....Remove the wooden beam from your eye first; then you will see clearly to remove the splinter from your brother's eye."

Matthew 7:1-2, 5

Prayer

Lord Jesus, you came not to judge the world, but to save the world. Teach me to see others as you see them and to love them as you love them.

Amen

The Teaching

Judgment of others sets us up for judgment: a harsh look at the world will conclude with God's judgment on us. It also means exalting oneself into the place reserved for God.

Few people will admit to being judgmental. "Judgies" will usually confess to all seven deadly sins before they finally stumble to a mirror and say, "Okay. I carp and criticize. I condemn and judge the people around me."

Most "judgies" know they tend to be perfectionists, but they hold that quality up as desirable. Some insist that they're just "impatient with stupidity," overlooking the fact that they had to judge someone stupid before they got impatient. "Judgies" comment on how the meeting could have been handled—even though they weren't there personally. They find fault with every menu your club ever planned and tell you how their old parish managed their Christmas bazaar with greater success. They usually have something to say about the way Father preaches, trains the altar boys, or celebrates Mass.

"Judgies" drive their coworkers nuts, often taking projects from others to show how it's supposed to be done "the right way." They're quick to judge others as "helpless" and "inept."

"Judgies" are even dangerous. They create desperately unhappy families, keeping their children miserable and their spouses nervous and furtive. Everyone tries to keep from incurring the wrath of "the judge." "Judgies" can destroy the persons they say they love most—all in the name of being helpful.

Scripture offers a wealth of teaching on judgmentalism. In the Book of Job, for example, Job's three judgmental friends assume he has committed some wrongdoing. They insist that Job suffers because the Lord is angry at him. Job has to confess his guilt, they say, before his health will be restored.

Job 42:7-9 focuses our attention on God's participation in Job's life. God speaks to Eliphaz, one of Job's so-called friends: "I am _____ with you and with your two friends; for you _____

_____, as has my servant Job."

Does God reward Job's judges in this situation? _____

Does God reward Job in this situation? _____

Why was God angry at Job's "friends"?

_____

_____

Who interceded for the three "comforters" so God would forgive them? _____

Jehoshaphat, one of the great godly kings of Israel, goes out to evangelize the people in the desert and highlands. Following the instructions of Moses, he appoints mediators for the people, to settle land disputes or infractions of the law.

The Second Book of Chronicles 19:4-6 emphasizes the importance of fairness. Jehoshaphat "appointed _____ in the land, in all the fortified cities of _____, city by city, and he said to them: 'Take care what you do, for you are _____, not on behalf of _____, but on behalf of the _____; he _____ with you.' "

Why is it important for the judges to be fair and careful?

_____

What do you think Jehoshaphat means when he says that the Lord judges "with you"?

_____

How does that apply to you today?

_____

_____

_____

In Luke 6:36-38, Jesus again calls for a nonjudgmental position. Jesus says, "Be _____, just as [also] your _____ is _____. Stop _____ and you will not be _____. Stop _____ and you will not be _____. Forgive and you will be _____."

How does this make praying for your enemies spiritually important?

_____

_____

What do you think happens when you pray for pardon while you are still in a state of judging someone?

_____

_____

John 8:3-10 recounts an incident that gives Jesus an opportunity to comment on judgment. When a woman is caught in a capital offense, Jesus chooses the way of love rather than judgment. The scribes and Pharisees lead the woman forward and make her stand in front of everyone. They say to Jesus, " 'Teacher, this woman was caught in the very act of committing _____. Now in the law, _____ commanded us to stone such women. So what do you say?' They said this to _____ him, so that they could have some charge to bring against him. Jesus bent down and began to _____ on the _____ with his finger. But when they continued asking him, he straightened up and said to them, 'Let the one among you who is without _____ be the first to _____.' "

Of course, no one throws anything, and Jesus and the woman are left alone. Jesus asks the woman if anyone has accused her. When she says, "No one, Sir," Jesus says, (v. 11) "_____ do I condemn you" (v. 11).

What do you think Jesus writes on the ground?

_____

_____

Why did all the woman's accusers disappear?

_____

_____

   This theme of compassion, pardon, forgiveness, and universal sinfulness continues in the Letter to the Romans. In 14:10, Paul asks, "Why then do you _____ your brother? Or you, why do you _____ on your brother? For we shall all stand before the _____ of God." According to this Scripture, how should knowing we will be judged by the Lord change our judgments of others?

_____

_____

_____

How can we change the way God judges us? (v. 12)

_____

_____

   The peppery Letter of James uses strong language to remind us that God is the only Lawgiver and Judge. Read 4:11-12. "Do not _____ of one another, brothers. Whoever speaks evil of a _____ or _____ his brother speaks evil of the law and judges the law....There is one _____ and _____ who is able to save or to destroy. Who then are you to judge your _____?"

Do you ever engage in judgmental gossip about friends, relatives, coworkers, or neighbors? What are some judgments you've made, aloud or in your heart, about others?

_____

_____

_____

_____

Is gossip a sin? Why or why not?

_____

_____

_____

_____

Is an individual harmed by criticism, judgment, or gossip that he or she never hears? Why or why not?

_____

_____

_____

How does it harm you to be critical of others?

_____

_____

_____

How do you feel when you hear that someone has judged or criticized you?

_____

_____

_____

_____

_____

Steps Toward a Nonjudgmental Life

Recovery from being a "judgie" isn't an overnight event; it's a fairly painful process. Recovery is also necessary to make yourself fit for the kingdom of heaven.

The following steps will help you along the way:

Recognize your sin. The Bible and the Church make it clear that judgmentalism is a sin. It's not a personality quirk or an irreversible tendency toward perfectionism; it isn't an inevitable part of an A-type personality. Judging others—even if you just call it impatience or helpfulness—is a sin. It's a form of arrogance and pride—the very sin that drove the Enemy out of heaven. Judging means you consider yourself superior in some way to another human being—and any form of superiority is forbidden by God.

Confess your sin to God; if possible, celebrate the sacrament of reconciliation. How does this realization make you feel?

Feelings _____

_____

_____

_____

Record the date you began to recognize your sinfulness.

Date _____

Ask for God's help. You can't overcome hardened and practiced judgmentalism alone; you need help just to know when you do it. Once you've started to recognize your sin, ask God to help you overcome it. Write your prayer here.

_____

_____

_____

_____

_____

Copy this prayer on an index card and place it where you'll see it every day.

Do some acts of goodness toward those you've judged. Send greeting cards to the people you've been carping about. Visit with them, taking a small token of thoughtfulness. If, for some reason, these persons are not on your Blessing List, include them and begin working on the forgiveness process. If you see these persons often, compliment them in some way, honestly and sincerely. Note these persons' names and the acts of goodness you perform toward them.

Person	Act of Goodness	Date
_____	_____	___
_____	_____	___
_____	_____	___
_____	_____	___
_____	_____	___
_____	_____	___
_____	_____	___

Begin to bless these persons. Go over this list (or your original blessing list) every day, and ask God to bless these persons, according to the method in Chapter Three.

Note the date when you begin this process.

Date _____

Every time you find yourself being judgmental, say out loud, "I'm sorry, God. Forgive me for judging." Even if you're in a roomful of family, friends, clergy, children, or business associates, do this. This step may "cure" you quicker than any other. Note the occasion and date you started to be judgmental and had to confess it publicly.

Occasion	Date
_____	_____
_____	_____
_____	_____
_____	_____

Use the journal pages at the end of this chapter if more space is needed.

Memorize some instructions. Commit to memory the following Bible passages and repeat them to yourself at least once daily: Matthew 7:1; Luke 6:37; Romans 14:10. Write them on index cards and tape them to your refrigerator, your bathroom mirror, or the inside cover of this book. Note the date when you begin memorizing and have successfully memorized each passage. Matthew 7:1

Begin memorizing _____

Successfully memorized _____

Luke 6:37

Begin memorizing _____

Successfully memorized _____

Romans 14:10

Begin memorizing _____

Successfully memorized _____

Ask someone close to you to tell you (or signal in some way) when you're speaking in a judgmental way. This is a hard one, but when you confess to a friend or your spouse that you've been judgmental, you may find that they've noticed. It isn't going to be easy to submit to another's help, but God sees your desire to change and will help you. Who is your helpful friend?

_____

Note the occasions when others have helped you with judgmentalism.

_____

_____

_____

For further personal and spiritual growth, borrow or buy a copy of C.S. Lewis's *The Great Divorce*. This slender book tells the story of a man who is privileged to glimpse the arrival of souls from purgatory (or hell, if they chose to return) into heaven. Chapter Nine contains a telling portrait: the Ghost of a woman whose judgmental "helping" had nearly destroyed those she "loved." After a particularly strong outburst, "...the Ghost which had towered up like a dying candle flame snapped suddenly. A sour, dry smell lingered in the air for a moment, and then there was no Ghost to be seen."

Journal

_____

_____

_____

_____

_____

_____

_____

_____

_____

_____

_____

_____

_____

_____

_____

_____

_____

_____

_____

_____

8.

The Sword and the Cross

Let them grow together until harvest; then at harvest time I will
say to the harvesters, "First collect the weeds and tie them in
bundles for burning; but gather the wheat into my barn."

Matthew 13:30

Prayer

Grant me, O God of peace, the ability to recognize
errors within the Church, to understand which of
them I should fight against and which I need to leave
to your judgment. May I know the joy of your presence in all things.

Amen

The Teaching

Although you must always be on guard against heresy
and maintain the Church's guardianship of the faith,
you can still leave judgment to God.

Learning not to be judgmental does not mean you quit caring
about social justice or that you tolerate evil. A person of blessing, a
nonjudgmental man or woman who is steeped in Christian forgiveness and the love of God, does not remain passive in the face of
starvation or abuse. Christ has an active Enemy in the world; evil
and error spill into every aspect of life, including the Church.

But God is on the throne. As you grow in the grace of blessing and forgiving, you will find ways to let God do what God does best, to let God take the kind of action that heals and restores.

Becoming God's Instrument

The following self-quiz will help you determine if you are fit for battle against God's enemies, if you know where and how to "take up arms."

Respond honestly to each statement by circling A, B, C, or D. Record your responses here or in your notebook. No one will see your responses except you. If none of the answers apply to you, check the ones you would like most to have apply if you were able to carry them out.

Part I: Christian Action

Circle the letter next to the statement that is closest to your situation.

A. I am fairly active in my church, school, and/or community.

B. I'm involved with issues I wish the Church would confront more vigorously.

C. I don't participate in parish council or any similar activities because they always end up in a fight.

D. I don't have any causes or strong opinions.

Part II: Involvement

Circle the letter next to the statement that is closest to the way you feel about your role in the Church.

I would like to see the entire Church more involved in
  A. peace and justice issues
  B. publicly fighting abortion
  C. mending the divisions between denominations
  D. not sure

God has called me
  A. to feed the hungry and help the poor
  B. to be an activist, fighting against moral injustices like abortion and capital punishment
  C. to make others happy at home, at work, and at church
  D. not sure

If I could, I would serve God and the Church
  A. in Latin America
  B. all over the United States
  C. by making others happy right here in my own home and parish
  D. not sure

If I were to grade the Church on how it is handling my concerns, I'd give it
  A. an A at home and a C in some other countries
  B. a poor grade in fighting hard against what's important
  C. an A- or B+ at the lowest
  D. I think most people in the Church do their best

Part III: Personality

Circle the letter next to the statement that best reflects your personality. If you can't find yourself, check the one that you'd like to be the closest or check "don't know."

I would describe my personality as
- A. fairly assertive, but not always the pacesetter
- B. very determined; when I decide to do something, nothing gets in my way
- C. agreeable; I like to get along with others, and I want to serve God as well as I can
- D. I can't analyze myself very well. I don't really know

Part IV: The Church and the World

Circle the letter next to the statement that best reflects the way you feel.

In general, the world
- A. is full of hurting people who need our help
- B. is full of evil and must be changed
- C. is still God's world, no matter what ·
- D. is something I don't understand very well

If I try my hardest,
- A. many things will still be left unresolved until the whole system changes
- B. our side can win
- C. people will get along better
- D. I might be able to help, but I don't know where or how

The Church's enemies
- A. are everywhere, including right at home
- B. need to be vanquished
- C. are something Christians shouldn't fight among themselves about
- D. aren't any of my business

If our Lord, Jesus Christ returned today, I would feel
- A. guilty for all I have not done
- B. proud of what I've tried to do
- C. joyful that all strife and sorrow would end
- D. I have no idea how I would feel, but the idea is a little scary

Part V: The Enemies

Circle the statement that best reflects what you believe.

I think the Church's major enemies are
- A. fear, prejudice, ignorance, and poverty
- B. abortionists, secular humanists, and New Age-ers
- C. those who destroy peace (include myself)
- D. I'm not qualified to judge

Scoring Code

If most of your answers are A, you're probably known as a liberal. You are generous and merciful toward everyone, including the needy and the oppressed. You would make a good fieldworker for the Church. You want to see mercy and justice done all over the world, but you may occasionally be impatient and even short-tempered with others' neglect of these causes. You may be frustrated with the Church's lack of direction and movement to resolve these problems. You tend to spread yourself too thin because so many causes are calling for your time and attention.

To serve the Church in the magnificent way you're called to serve, decide on one or two areas where you can be effective and let God find others to take care of the rest.

If most of your answers are A, note ways you are now serving or areas in which you'd like to serve.

_____

_____

_____

_____

If most of your answers are B, you're a go-getter, someone with terrific energy and a spirit of certainty. You've read that the gates of hell will not prevail against you, and you're determined to watch them fall. You have powerful opinions, and you're willing to stand behind them—even to the point of going to jail. You also have a tendency to be somewhat judgmental. You may inadvertently walk over others to pursue your cause. When you begin with love for Christ and his Church, there's no stopping you!

If most of your responses are B, note ways you can be a more effective and less abrasive servant.

_____

_____

_____

_____

If most of your responses are C, you're a pleasure to have around; you've never had a real fight with a friend, and you're the first one to give in if there's an argument. You would and probably have literally given the shirt off your back to someone you care about. Unfortunately, unless you are a true saint, your fear of "trouble" has made you the least important person in your own life. You may be the adult child of an alcoholic or a codependent in a dysfunctional home. Whatever has lowered your own self-esteem and made you scared of a fight, get rid of it—and you'll truly become one of God's great peacemakers.

If most of your responses are C, note ways you can be more important in your own life and of truer service to God.

If most of your answers are D, hello! Is anybody home? You may have a terrific faith, but you aren't sure how to act on it. In fact, you don't even know yourself well, do you. You may be an adult survivor of child abuse, a battered spouse, or someone who was always told to shut up and listen. Whatever the reason for your condition, get whatever kind of help you need. Grow toward being the open and loving person God means for you to be.

If most of your responses are D, note the ways you'd like to serve God in the Church. List steps you can take toward that goal.

If your answers are an even mixture, pick the dominant letter, even if it's a small majority; that's probably who you'd like to be or the way you'd like to serve God in the Church. If your responses are a balanced mixture, you're not sure who you are—or you're not being quite honest with yourself. Are you scared of your answers? Are you spread out over all these personality types? If so, it's time you choose a direction. Only with direction can you be an effective part of the Church's action.

The Wheat and the Weeds

Jesus tells a parable about the mixture of evil and good in the world. Read Matthew 13:24-30.

Who does the man symbolize in this parable?

_____

What kind of seed does he sow?

_____

Who does the enemy symbolize?

_____

What does the enemy sow in the field?

_____

What or whom do these weeds represent?

_____

Who do you think are the sower's "slaves" or servants?

_____

Why didn't they pull the weeds out of the wheat before they grew large?

_____

What does the harvest represent?

_____

What do the barn and the burning symbolize?

_____

_____

What does this parable teach about evildoers, God's enemies, and the Church's duty toward them?

_____

_____

_____

_____

What is Jesus saying to you today in the parable?

_____

_____

_____

Where do you see yourself in this parable?

_____

_____

How can you put the teachings of this parable into practice in your own life?

_____

_____

_____

It's easy to forget that in the process of pulling the weeds out of the Church and our society, we risk injuring the tender wheat plants.

List three "weeds" or enemies of Christian life, and then pray for those three daily. If they're already on your Blessing List (page 24), note special persons or groups within those categories who need prayer. For instance, if you're praying for pornographers, find out the name of a particular editor of the magazine you find offensive. If you're worried about free birth control products being handed out in schools, pray over the name of the school nurse.

1. _____

2. _____

3. _____

Journal

_____

_____

_____

_____

_____

_____

_____

_____

_____

_____

_____

_____

_____

_____

_____

_____

_____

_____

_____

_____

9.

Blessed Are the Peacemakers

"Again, [amen,] I say to you, if two of you agree on earth about anything for which they are to pray, it shall be granted to them by my heavenly Father."

Matthew 18:19

Prayer

Dear God, give us a spirit of peace and a great love for others, that we may truly become the Church that Christ established.

Amen

The Teaching

We might want to change the world, but we also need change from within: within the Church, within our homes, and within ourselves.

As you work through this chapter, keep Pogo's comment in mind: "We have met the enemy, and he is us."

The nun nods her head as she listens to parish council members discuss their problems. They tell her about financial hardship and the need for bigger and newer buildings. They offer a hundred reasons why parish dreams haven't been fulfilled. With a calm reserve, the nun says, "None of these is the problem. The real problem is that you're all at one another's throats."

Sister Mary Benet, O.S.B., prioress of her Benedictine community in Chicago, is a conflict-resolution specialist. She flies all over the country teaching church workers how to get along. She reminds groups that at one time Catholics didn't have—and didn't expect to have—any authority in their parishes. The pastor made all the decisions. After the Second Vatican Council, however, changes in the structure of the Church meant that laypeople, for the first time, were to take responsibility for much that went on in schools and parish life. Despite this new responsibility and privilege, however, laypeople had no idea how to get along.

"In fact," Sister Mary Benet says, "nothing is more destructive to Christian relationships than the average board meeting."

Most of us agree. We know that, as Pogo has so eloquently stated, the enemy is us. But even people of blessing and forgiveness have trouble understanding where change needs to start.

Why Groups Have Internal Problems

How can Christian groups learn to get along while they make hard decisions? Check all responses below that reflect your feelings. All these statements were gathered from real people in real situations.

_____ Groups can get along if they meticulously follow parliamentary procedure.

_____ Infighting reflects lack of trust. If distrust is eliminated through understanding, a group can learn to get along.

_____ Things run better when one person is in charge of everything.

_____ Committees should handle things and report to the larger body.

_____ Men are better than women when it comes to maintaining order.

_____ No decision should be made unless all members agree.

_____ Voting on an issue always makes someone feel left out.

_____ Voting on an issue is the way democracy works best.

_____ The reason groups fall apart is because they don't listen to the leader. Leaders always know what's best for the group.

_____ Groups erupt into backbiting subgroups because they have no idea how to be cohesive.

_____ Group infighting is caused by control issues and power struggles between the people involved.

_____ Groups dissolve because of the tyranny of the minority.

_____ If you're part of a group minority, your voice will never be heard.

Bringing Christ Into the Church

Sometimes it looks as if Christ is everywhere except in the Church. Group infighting, factions, and divisions in the Body of Christ have gone on since the beginning. The first big argument had to do with whether gentile Christian men had to be circumcised and adhere to the Mosaic Law. James, Bishop of the Jerusalem Church, called a synod of apostles and presbyters to decide the issue.

Chapter 5 of Paul's letter to the Galatians gives us a great deal of special insight into the struggles for peace and unity within the early Church. Read verses 13-15; concentrate on what Paul says: "For you were called for _____....But do not use this freedom as an opportunity for the _____." Paul points out that serving others through love fulfills the law to love others as you love yourself. He pinpoints what is at risk (v. 15): "But if you go on _____ and _____ one another, beware that you are _____ by one another."

In verses 19-21, Paul says, "Now the works of the _____ are obvious: immorality, impurity, licentiousness, idolatry, sorcery, _____, _____, _____, _____ of _____, _____ of _____, _____, _____, _____ of _____, _____ _____, _____, and the like."

Note that Paul places dissension and factions in the same sin-class as idolatry, sorcery, and immorality. Did you know that? How does that make you feel?

_____

_____

_____

If even the first apostles had personality clashes and struggles over principle, what are modern Christians to do? Paul continues to give us guidance in verses 22-23: "In contrast, the _____ of the _____ is _____, _____, _____, _____, _____, _____, _____, _____, _____, _____, _____.

Against such, there is no law."

These nine fruits of the Holy Spirit are sometimes not in evidence at a parish council or building committee meeting. But Sister Mary Benet has some suggestions. "The first thing to do is get rid of parliamentary procedure. Quit voting when you make decisions."

Her audiences always gasps at these words. How can an organization survive without orderly procedure, without voting on issues?

"When you vote, someone wins and someone loses," she explains. "That means someone's happy and someone else is probably mad."

But isn't that unavoidable? Just part of life?

"Christians should be able to make no-lose decisions. Or else they should make no decision at all." Part of Sister Mary Benet's ministry includes teaching councils and boards—and anyone else who wants to find a new way for groups to function—how to make decisions by consensus, unanimous agreement.

"Quakers have been working by consensus for two hundred years," she says. "No wonder they like one another so well. And decisions or elections in most monasteries work on consensus."

Decision by Consensus

Sister Mary Benet's steps in decision making for groups of any size begin with presenting the possible decision. For instance, let's say you're on the school board at your local Catholic high school, and the vice principal is leaving. You've interviewed nine people for the vice principal's job, and you're down to three possible candidates. Or perhaps your parish is considering a new policy for operating a soup kitchen, and opinions differ widely among the parishioners.

Make a covenant with yourself and the group not to rush the process, no matter how short time seems. Decide to wait on the will of God for your decision. Then use the following steps to reach a decision. Keep a record of this process; fill in the blanks as you come to those steps.

If there is hostility within the group, try to have an outside arbitrator conduct the meetings. If the waters are troubled even before you start the decision process, or if a small vocal group has expressed its intention of "winning," bring in a person not connected to the school or parish. This can be someone from a parish outside the city or from a nearby college or industry. Make sure, however, that the person uses the process as it is outlined below.

Note the date when you and your group begin this process.

Date _____

1. After a prayer for the Holy Spirit's guidance, let the advocates for each position, candidate, or opinion present themselves without any expression of opposition from the rest of the group. Set a time limit and enforce it; record these positions. No interruptions or sounds of approval or displeasure are allowed. The recorder can write the major opinions on a sheet of newsprint, a blackboard, or an overhead projector sheet. For yourself, note here the major opinions presented and the number of people who participate in the consensus-discernment process.

Opinion _____

_____

Opinion _____

_____

Opinion _____

_____

Opinion _____

_____

Number of people participating in the process _____

2. Let every person present express his or her opinion for a specified amount of time (five minutes, for example). Nobody may interrupt or express opposition. Record these opinions in the same manner selected in the first step. Be sure that even the

shyest person is heard if he or she has something to say. Give everyone a chance to speak. Insist that others listen without verbal or nonverbal expressions of opinion.

What is your opinion of the process up to this point?

_____

_____

_____

_____

_____

3. One more time, allow everyone present to add or subtract from his or her original statements. Continue this activity without interruptions from others. Limit this time to two minutes per person. Record these changes. This is each person's opportunity to express what he or she may have left out, forgotten, or thought of after hearing other comments. It is not time for argument or rebuttal.

4. Ask if anyone wants to add to or disagree with statements made by others. Limit the time, and do not allow interruptions. This is a time for listening, not arguing.

How do you feel about the process up to this point?

_____

_____

_____

_____

_____

5. Allow members to raise their hands and ask questions of other members. Still, no argument is permitted. This is an exercise in clarification. It is a time to be sure everyone understands and feels understood.

6. Ask if anyone feels that his or her opinion was not heard or understood. Leaving even one person out of the decision-making exercise generates distrust. If the group is large, take a coffee break at this point. You may even suggest that the meeting be adjourned and a second meeting scheduled to continue with the process. Ask that everyone refrain from "lobbying" one another.

7. Have the person serving as recorder set up a simple chart showing all the opinions. By now, most ideas have probably drawn together into two to five basic opinions. If you have time, run them off on a copier; otherwise, continue to use newsprint.

8. Once again, pray for the guidance of the Holy Spirit. Take a consensus check (not a vote). Find out how many people subscribe to each position. If everyone already agrees, you can stop the process; the decision is made! However, if your group is like most, you probably need to continue.

When you and your group finish this portion of the process, record your feelings. How do you think the process is going?

_____

_____

_____

How do you feel about your participation in the process?

_____

_____

9. Repeat Steps 1 through 8. If a great number of dissention remains within the group, table the decision. You've prayed for God's guidance; either that guidance isn't forthcoming yet or someone isn't listening. Hire an interim principal or put off the soup kitchen for at least a month, then repeat the entire process. Don't enter into a decision when feelings are hurt and Christian unity is injured.

If a consensus check reveals that only one or two people disagree, continue with the next step. In no way should any group member be allowed to express disapproval toward these few persons or their ideas.

10. When one or two people still hold out against the group, ask for their help in enlightening the others. The convener should turn to these people and say with sincerity, "Obviously, you know something about this (candidate, situation, and so forth) we don't. Can you help us understand that?"

11. After the few dissenters have offered their help or advice, pray for the guidance of the Holy Spirit by keeping a few minutes of silence. Then, once again, take a consensus check. It may have changed. It's possible that these people just needed to be heard better, and that your willingness to listen made them change their position. It's also possible that the rest of the group will swing to the minority position.

Note the results of the process and how you feel about any decision made.

---

12. If the consensus hasn't changed, repeat Steps 4 through 6. If one or two holdouts still remain, ask for their assent. Someone may need to take a walk with a person who can't agree, to see if he or she feels pressured or blackmailed into agreement. If that person's position is basically a difference of opinion, ask, "Can you go along with this, even if you don't agree with it?"

13. Repeat Step 9. You should either have an agreeable consensus or a tabled decision. God is never in a hurry; groups shouldn't be, either.

Make some final notes about the decision. What decision was reached?

_____

_____

_____

_____

Record the date the decision was reached.

Date _____

How long did the group process take? _____

How do you feel about the other group members now? (Do you still need to work on being nonjudgmental?)

_____

_____

_____

_____

_____

Will the consensus model change the Church? Given enough time and a wide enough range of activity, it can. Meanwhile, if you—and thousands of others—are blessing your enemies and forgiving your friends for their shortcomings, you probably won't have any problems when you get to the board meeting and participate in creating a consensus.

Journal

10.

Your Gift at the Altar

"If you bring your gift to the altar, and there recall that your brother has anything against you, leave your gift there at the altar, go first and be reconciled with your brother...."

Matthew 5:23-24

Prayer

Lord, teach us how to be reconcilers, to soften the anger of those around us, and to be willing to sacrifice ourselves for the sake of holiness.

Amen

The Teaching

All our gifts to God—service to the Church, charitable works, and our offerings—may be valueless if we have not made peace with our enemies.

What gifts do you bring to the Christian community? Do you tithe your time, talents, and/or money, giving a certain percentage of your income and your free hours to the work of the parish or to some relief agency? Are you involved with retreats, liturgy planning, youth ministry, parish administration, or catechetics? Using the guide below, check the gifts you offer God and estimate the quantity.

_____ I tithe or give a fixed pledge or percentage of my income to my parish: $_____ per week

_____ I donate financial gifts to national church activities: $_____ per year

_____ I make financial gifts to charity: $_____ per year

_____ I do volunteer work at church: _____ hours per month

_____ I assist in church activities (music, eucharistic ministry, lector, usher, RCIA instructor, CCD teacher, home caller, hospital minister): _____ hours per month

_____ I volunteer at a parochial school: _____ hours per month

_____ I do volunteer work in my community: _____ hours per month

_____ I do full-time work (paid or volunteer) in church, parochial school, or other Christian activities: _____ hours per month

_____ I make other contributions/offer other services:

_____

_____

_____

_____

_____

Notice what Matthew's Gospel says about the gifts we bring to the altar: 5:23-24. "If you bring your gift to the _____, and there recall that your _____ has anything _____ you, _____ your gift there at the _____, go first and ____ _____ with your _____, and then come and _____ your gift." Notice that the passage does not say

"If you hold anything against your brother" but says "If your brother has anything _____ _____."

Does that mean anyone who is upset at you or just those with whom you might be able to make peace?

_____

What does this passage imply about your gifts to church and charity?

_____

_____

_____

_____

Is there someone who holds something against you or is hurt or angry at you (justly or otherwise)? List their names below.

_____   _____

_____   _____

_____   _____

Which of these people are on your Blessing List?

_____   _____

_____   _____

_____   _____

When the ancient practice of passing the peace was restored to the Mass (the sign of peace), some of us struggled against it.

Some of us even balked. We didn't like the idea of shaking hands (let alone hugging) the strangers and near-strangers in the pews around us. Imagine if the priest interrupted Mass just before Communion and sent us out, as in this Scripture reading, to make peace with our enemies. What if the priest insisted that we do what Jesus said: go be reconciled not with those who have angered you but with those who—justly or unjustly—are mad at you?

It might take days or even weeks before Mass could be resumed, not because we have so many enemies but because most of us have not learned *how to be forgiven*. We can ask God to forgive us; we can celebrate the sacrament of reconciliation. But in personal relationships, most of us like to be the one who does the forgiving.

God wants us to be whole people who participate in both sides of forgiveness: forgiving and being forgiven. The reading from Matthew tells us that the gifts we bring may be worthless in God's sight until we seek forgiveness.

Which of the following statements answers the question "Why did Jesus give us this teaching?" (Check any answers you think apply.)

_____ God wants the whole world to be at peace.

_____ God knows we can't offer our gifts wholeheartedly when someone is angry with us.

_____ If someone is holding something against us, we're not really at peace ourselves.

_____ It isn't good for our "enemies" to hold grudges against us; God wants us to be instruments of redemption for those persons.

_____ We'll feel better about life if we make peace with our brothers and sisters.

_____ God can forgive us best when we are both forgiving and forgiven.

Making the First Move

Most of us have at least one "enemy" who thinks we owe an apology. Maybe you're waiting for such a person to apologize to you first. You both may be waiting for the other to make the first move.

That was Rachel's situation. Her teenage daughter's boyfriend, Rick, had broken a serious rule at Rachel's house, and she ordered him to leave and not return. Her daughter was brokenhearted, talking several times a day on the phone to the boy and crying inconsolably. But Rachel was adamant: the boy had misbehaved and that was that.

Meanwhile, Rick grew angry at Rachel. What right did she have to keep him away from the girl he loved and wanted to marry?

Rachel and her family sat on the opposite side of their Episcopal church from Rick and his parents. Both families could see that the other did not receive the Body and Blood for more than three months: each bore an unforgiven sin on his or her heart and was afraid to approach the Lord's altar.

One Sunday the gospel reading was Matthew 5:23-24. As the bell rang for Communion, Rick started out the back of church, as he'd done for three months. That morning, however, Rachel tiptoed to the back and grabbed Rick's hand.

"Come on, Rick," she said. "Let's go receive Communion together."

Rick started to cry and whispered, "I'm sorry"; but Rachel shook her head. Jesus' words were ringing in her head, and she wanted desperately to obey them. "Let's just forget it," she said, and they approached the altar together.

Rick married Rachel's daughter. They recently celebrated their twenty-fifth anniversary, and Rick is one of Rachel's best friends.

Would it be possible for you to make amends to the people

(on your list on previous page) who are hurt or angry with you? What could you say to make things better? Can you write a letter, make a phone call, or go visit these people? How would you ask them to forgive you? What you would like to say to them, in writing or in person?

_____

_____

_____

_____

_____

_____

_____

_____

_____

_____

If any of these are "enemies" on your Blessing List, continue your prayers of blessing for them. If not, begin today to bless these people for at least a week before you consider asking for forgiveness. Record the date when you begin saying prayers of blessing for these persons.

Date _____

If you decide to ask someone for forgiveness, or to make amends, record the date you decide to take this step.

Date _____

How do you feel about this decision?

_____

_____

_____

_____

Record the names of the people with whom you try to become reconciled, the date you wrote or visited them, and the outcome.

Name	Date	Outcome

What if the person you call or write has an angry outburst and accuses you unjustly? Read Matthew 5:25, the verse following the passages above. Jesus gives special guidelines about being forgiven. "Settle with your opponent _____ while on the way to _____ with him." The wording in *King James Bible* is slightly different, and perhaps a little more direct: "Agree with your adversary quickly, while you are in the way with him."

Agree? Does that sound outrageous when another person may be attacking you without cause? What if you try to reestablish communication with your sister, who has made you miserable all your life, or a former business partner, who covers his or her own ineptitude by accusing you of theft?

Notice that Jesus doesn't say "Become best friends with your opponent." He says to agree with your adversary, to make peace. As far as you are able, to the extent that the situation depends on you, reach out to anyone who holds anything against you. The "court" is the court of God's kingdom.

In Matthew 5:38-41, Jesus offers further direction. "You have heard that it was said, 'An _____ for an _____ and a _____ for a _____.' But I say to you, offer no _____ to one who is _____. When someone _____ you on [your] _____ _____, turn the _____ one to him as well. If anyone wants to go to _____ with you over your _____, hand him your _____ as well. Should anyone press you into service for _____, go with him for _____." (In the culture of Jesus' day, a Roman soldier could randomly—and sometimes brutally—force a citizen to carry his pack or other belongings.)

This is hard to accept. Does God really expect us to treat one another this way? to kowtow to our enemies? to abandon self-respect?

God wants us to behave in a courteous and self-sacrificing way not just to benefit our enemies but to benefit ourselves. Our goodness shows our enemies what the kingdom of God is really about. Jesus' words aren't about neurotic self-sacrifice or low self-esteem. We all know people who can't stand up for themselves if their lives depend on it, who wear "Kick me" on every cell of their being. We know people who have been so abused as children that now they're perpetual victims. Jesus' words are not about such people. They're meant for those who can consciously and willingly decide to give up their own desires to carry out God's will.

When Susan was a small child, she reached through her neighbor's fence and pulled up a huge bunch of bright, colorful flowers. She also broke stems, pulled up some tender roots, and left a gaping hole in the garden. Knowing what she'd done wasn't right, she rushed home, gave her mother the flowers, and said she found them.

Before long, the elderly lady who owned the garden came to the door and asked Susan's mother if she had a little girl who could have pulled out her flowers. Sadly, the mother called her child to come apologize.

"I didn't come here for an apology," the old lady said. "I came to show you what to do when you want some flowers." She pulled a pair of scissors from her pocket and added, "Let's go cut a bouquet. A girl smart enough to love flowers is smart enough to learn how to cut them properly."

Susan never forgot that incident, nor did her mother. It was a perfect example of self-giving love, of forgiveness, of turning a sinful act into a blessing.

Does that remind you of anything about our Lord, Jesus Christ? Read what Paul tells us about the redemptive grace of Jesus in Romans 3:23-24. "All have _____ and are deprived of the _____ of _____. They are _____ freely by his grace through the _____ in Christ Jesus."

In other words, we don't deserve the sacrifice of Christ; we don't deserve God's forgiveness. No matter how good we are, we can't be good enough to deserve forgiveness. The cross is not only a sign of God's love but a reminder that even the unjust can be forgiven—sometimes (like Susan) even before they ask.

How about your gifts at the altar? Do you need to go make peace with someone before you offer them, even someone who doesn't deserve it?

Journal

_____

_____

_____

_____

_____

_____

_____

_____

_____

_____

_____

_____

_____

_____

_____

_____

_____

_____

11.
Continuing Toward Inner Peace

You've been on a journey. Unlike a vacation, however, this journey doesn't end with piles of laundry, shoes full of sand, and suitcases to be unpacked. In fact, it doesn't end at all.

Once you start blessing your enemies and forgiving your friends, you don't stop. Once you let God get a toehold in your inner life, you might as well give up. God wants everything, not just an occasional prayer for your ailing friend or a grateful thought at a bountiful table.

Note the changes you've seen in yourself as you've moved through the previous chapters.

_____

_____

_____

_____

_____

Reflecting on these changes, do you really want to end this journey? Aren't you more peaceful inside, more in harmony with the world you live in, even more comfortable with God than you were when you began? You've learned to

+ ferret out old grudges and angers
+ bless your enemies and pray that God will bringthem joy
+ unburden yourself of old resentments and other "anesthetics" for pain
+ forgive others who have wounded you
+ tame your tongue—for the sake of health
+ look at the Church's enemies in a new light
+ discern consensus
+ make peace before bringing your gifts to the altar

What other joys and insights do you imagine God has in store for you?

As you continue this journey, you'll want to take along several necessary things: your Bible, for example, and a plan or outline for reading it. You may want to consider following the *Lectionary;* it provides several readings every day. You may choose to read a devotional magazine like *My Daily Visitor* (available from Our Sunday Visitor, 200 Noll Plaza, Huntington, IN 46750) or *Forward Day by Day* (available from Forward Movement Publications, 412 Sycamore Street, Cincinnati, OH 45202). Catholic and other Christian bookstores carry one-year Bibles and other guides that can help you structure your Bible-reading time. You'll also want to take along your journal. In fact, you may need a new notebook by now. Continue to write prayers, record experiences, and develop new prayer lists.

Keep this book nearby and periodically review the processes you've learned. Each time you journey through this book, you do so as a new person with new insights, new ways of praying, and new levels of growth.

Remember the prayer from *The Dollmaker* that was quoted in Chapter Three? It's the Aaronic prayer of blessing found in Numbers 6:24-26. I leave it here as a blessing for you today. Before this day is finished, pass it on to just one other person.

The LORD bless you and keep you!
The LORD let his face shine upon you
  and be gracious to you!
The LORD look upon you kindly and give you peace!

Amen

More Ways to Find Peace and Inner Freedom...

How to Forgive Yourself and Others
Steps to Reconciliation
by Rev. Eamon Tobin

This best-selling booklet *How to Forgive Yourself and Others* still contains all of the helpful original material, but in this revised and expanded edition Father Tobin deals with other important issues of reconciliation, offers new guidelines for forgiving a deceased person, presents new sections on forgiving God and the Church, and has expanded his section on forgiveness of self. *$3.95*

Scripture-Based Solutions to Reaching Out to Others
by Pat King

This book contains ten lessons which study a variety of ways to reach out to others. By reflecting on Scripture and applying its wisdom to life, readers will discover how to reach out in genuine Christlike fashion. *$5.95*

The Beatitudes
Jesus' Pattern for a Happy Life
by Marilyn Gustin

In this book, Gustin invites readers to consider the beatitudes as a pattern for peace. By presenting a collection of suggestions and directions for experimentation in daily living, she offers a challenge to listen to Jesus' Sermon on the Mount—his way to face troubles and problems and still find peace, hope, and joy. *$4.95*